A Trip Down a River

by Linda Cernak
illustrated by Frank Riccio

Harcourt

Orlando   Boston   Dallas   Chicago   San Diego

Visit *The Learning Site!*

www.harcourtschool.com

Out west, there is a long river called the Colorado River. This river runs along the bottom of the Grand Canyon.

A canyon is a large valley that has been carved out of rock. It took many years for the Colorado River to form the Grand Canyon.

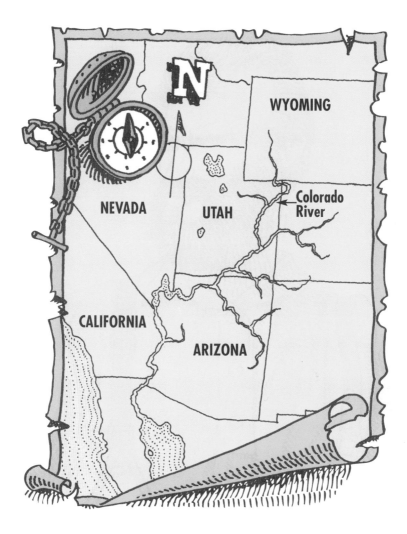

The Colorado River begins high in the mountains of Colorado. It flows through Utah and Arizona, and ends in Mexico. It connects with many rivers along the way.

Many years ago, there were no maps of the Colorado River. John Powell, a scientist, wanted to explore the river. He took nine other men with him on this trip.

Powell and his men began their journey
in Wyoming. Boats, food, and supplies were
sent there by train. Powell brought
notebooks so he could write about his trip
and make drawings. No mapmaker had yet
drawn a map of the whole river.

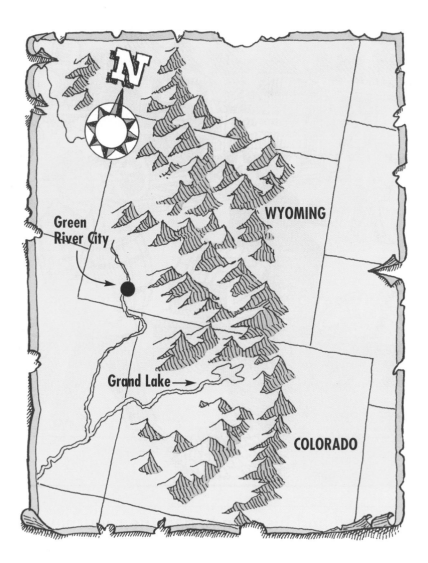

The trip started at Green River City, which is near the source of the Colorado River— Grand Lake in Colorado.

On May 11, the trip began. The boats pushed off onto the Green River. Powell's group had a long distance to go before the journey would end. The trip would take more than three months to finish.

The boats passed safely through a group
of three canyons. Powell sketched pictures
to show the features of the canyons.

Next, the men came to a waterfall. One of
the four boats broke apart at the falls. Food
and supplies were lost, too. Powell and his
men did not give up. The group bravely
moved on.

Powell and his group stopped to camp for a few days. They were tired and needed to rest so they made a campfire.

Some of their food had spoiled from the river water splashing into the boats. No one wanted to peel the potatoes or eat them, because they were rotten.

While the men ate dinner, a strong wind blew the fire onto a group of trees. A brush fire started and spread down the canyon.

All of the men rushed for their boats. They got ahead of the fire just in time! They were safe, traveling down the river once again.

Powell's expedition camped near the beginning of the Yampa River. The food supply continued to spoil because of the water, but the fishing was very good. The men were hopeful.

Later Powell and his men came to another river. There, six of them camped for a few days while Powell and three other men hiked a great distance into the woods.

The hikers met Native Americans who lived in the woods. The Native Americans gave Powell supplies to make up for the ones that were lost.

The trip down the river continued. Boats rode the rapids and bounced up and down. Powell fell out of his boat. He could not hold on and had to swim to the shore. John lost his bedding and some of his supplies.

Finally the river met up with the Grand River. Today we call it the Colorado River.

Powell and his men stopped to fix their boats and threw away spoiled food. Since this area was new to them, they used local maps to figure out where they were.

The trip down the river went on. The river's rapid water often was a problem. Sometimes the men rode through it. At other times, they moved the boats close to the shore and pulled them for a distance.

Already one man had given up the expedition. Near the end of the trip, three more men left because they were discouraged. Just two days later, Powell and the rest of the men finished their journey.

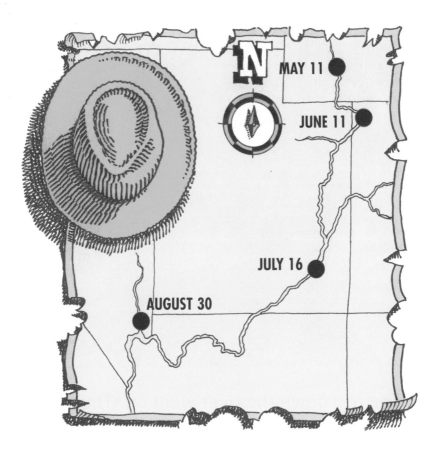

After more than three months of riding the river, they had come to the end of their trip. They had traveled more than 1,000 miles in 98 days!

Powell's journey was a tremendous success and helped Americans understand this western area of the country.